George Tierney

A Letter to the Right Hon. Henry Dundas

George Tierney

A Letter to the Right Hon. Henry Dundas

ISBN/EAN: 9783744689199

Printed in Europe, USA, Canada, Australia, Japan

Cover: Foto ©Thomas Meinert / pixelio.de

More available books at **www.hansebooks.com**

TO THE

RIGHT HON. HENRY DUNDAS,

PRESIDENT OF THE BOARD OF CONTROUL,

ON THE

STATEMENT OF THE AFFAIRS OF THE

EAST INDIA COMPANY,

LATELY PUBLISHED

BY GEORGE ANDERSON, ESQ.

ACCOUNTANT TO THE COMMISSIONERS FOR THE AFFAIRS OF INDIA.

BY GEORGE TIERNEY, ESQ.

LONDON:

PRINTED FOR J. DEBRETT, OPPOSITE BURLINGTON HOUSE, PICCADILLY.

1792.

Right Hon. HENRY DUNDAS.

ERRATA.

Page 43—For £ 13,248,673, read £ 13,258,673.
For £1,003,342, read £ 1,013,342.

The References to the Pages in Mr. Anderfon's
Publication are according to the laft Edition.

might be prefixed : perfonal refponfibility,
however, I never fhrunk from, having, on
all occafions, where queftioned, uniformly
acknowledged myfelf to be the writer of
that pamphlet which I now conceive I am
called upon in this more public manner
to avow.

After a hefitation of near twelve months,
you are pleafed to take up the gauntlet
which has fo long lain before you ; and, by

B   your

Right Hon. HENRY DUNDAS.

SIR,

IN the month of May, 1791, I took the liberty to addrefs to you a letter on the fubject of the Finances of the Eaft India Company. This letter, it is true, was not figned with my name, for I felt too ftrongly the infignificance of that name to fuppofe that, in the eftimation of the world, it could give weight to any ftatement to which it might be prefixed : perfonal refponfibility, however, I never fhrunk from, having, on all occafions, where queftioned, uniformly acknowledged myfelf to be the writer of that pamphlet which I now conceive I am called upon in this more public manner to avow.

After a hefitation of near twelve months, you are pleafed to take up the gauntlet which has fo long lain before you ; and, by

B   your

your fquire Mr. Anderfon, Accountant to
the Commiffioners for the Affairs of India,
you at laft come forward to accept a chal-
lenge of which the giver had almoft loft the
recollection. Your valour, Mr. Dundas,
has been fomewhat tardy, but it fhall not
be difappointed ; and, though I will confefs
that I had for fome time ceafed to expect
any fuch effort of refolution on your part,
I inftantly obey your fummons, and enter
the lifts.

I am called upon to defend two accounts ;
the *firft* of which Mr. Anderfon afferts to
abound with " grofs miftatements," leading
to conclufions " very different from the actual refult ;" and the *fecond* of which he
chufes to infinuate, contains a moft material
error, " committed for the purpofe of giving
" a ftatement that fhould apparently fup-
" port the inferences which it was previoufly
" intended to exhibit."

The firft account is the following——

GENERAL

GENERAL STATEMENT

Of the PROFIT and LOSS of the EAST INDIA COMPANY, for Four Years.

Dr.

To cost of cargoes shipped from India and China, in the seasons 1786-7, 1787-8, 1788-9, and 1789-90 inclusive to the invoices, for four years	£11,038,541
To commercial charges in India, exclusive of what added to the invoices, for four years	400,000
To tea purchased in Europe between the 1st of March 1787 and 1st of March 1791	179,508
To expences at St. Helena, four years, at 27,000l. per ann.	108,000
To charges in England, between the 1st of March 1787, and 1st March 1791	898,541
To cash advanced by the Paymaster of his Majesty's forces for troops serving in India, and repaid, or to be repaid, by the Company for the years 1787-8-9-90	290,483
To interest on debt transferred from India, due from 1st of March 1788 to the 1st of March 1791	188,637
To four years interest to Annuitants	360,000
To interest on bonds in England, from the 1st of March 1787 to 1st March 1791	438,000
To four years dividends from 1st March 1787, to the 1st of March 1791	1,440,000
	15,341,710
To loss on goods and stores exported from England to India and China, for four years	560,000
	15,901,710
Four years profit, *supposing the encreased stock on hand to produce what valued at by the Company*	2,152,505
	£18,054,215

Cr.

By encrease of goods on hand — Goods on hand 1st of March 1791	£4,343,031	
Deduct for goods on hand 1st March 1787	2,797,636	
		£1,545,395
By nett sales of goods from India and China, between the 1st of March 1787, and the 1st of March 1791		12,453,377
By profit on private trade during the same period		354,889
By four years interest received from government, being 3 per cent. on 4,800,000l.		94,000
		14,857,661
By four years nett surplus in India		3,196,554
		£18,054,215

On

On this ftatement Mr. Anderfon commences his attack in thefe words,——

"The nett furplus of India from 1786-7
"to 1789-90, is computed by this writer at
"£3,196,554. From the fame accounts
"it appears, in page 67 of the foregoing
"fheets, that the nett furplus amounted to
"£3,956,246; which, from the circum-
"ftances there explained, was not the
"whole fum which the refources of India
"had afforded to the purpofes of trade, &c.
"In making this computation, the writer
"ftates the whole intereft incurred on the
"debts in India as paid, and the whole
"of the charges *defrayed*, as incurred;
"whereas, very little of the intereft in-
"curred at Bombay (vide No. 5 of 24th of
"March, 1790, and the two Nos. 34 of
"1791) was paid in this period; but ar-
"rears there, and at the other fettlements,
"were paid to nearly an equal amount, and
"form a part of the charges *defrayed*. By
"not attending to this circumftance, he has
"charged near £700,000 too much againft
"the refources of India. This fum, and
"his having taken the revenues and charges
"of Bombay, in 1789-90, and the expences
"of

" of Bencoolen and Prince of Wales' Ifland
" on eftimate, accounts for the error of
" £759,692 in the article of Surplus Re-
" venue from India."

In anfwer to the laft part of this charge,
I admit that an error does arife from my
having taken the accounts of Bombay, Bencoolen, and Prince of Wales' Ifland on eftimate; but the reafon for my having fo done
will furely appear fatisfactory, when I bring
to your recollection, that at the time my
pamphlet was printed, no actual accounts
had been received, and there was nothing
but an eftimate to take. Previous, however,
to its publication authentic accounts did
come to hand, upon the receipt of which
I immediately prefixed an advertifement to
what I had written, ftating the fact, and
pointing out a miftake of £84,436 in my way
of giving the total furplus in India ;—and
this very fum is now brought againft me as
one of my " grofs miftatements." So much
for the candour of your accountant.

With refpect to the next head, namely,
my having ftated " the whole intereft in-
" curred on the debt in India as paid," I reply,

ply, that in examining the fituation of the Company with a view to afcertain the fair refult of their income and expenditure, I apprehend the method I adopted to have been perfectly correct. I affumed that the Company *received* what was annually due *to* them, and *paid* what was annually due *by* them, and I know of no other way by which the true value of an eftate can be afcertained. A man who has a thoufand a year, and lives at the rate of five hundred but neglects to difcharge his bills, furely cannot be faid to be a man of better fortune than his neighbour who, with the fame income, and the fame eftablifhment, regularly pays his tradefmen ; and yet I muft be brought to that way of thinking, before I can agree to alter my ftatement according to Mr. Anderfon's fuggeftion.

But, in truth, the difference between your accountant and me refpecting the Surplus Revenue in India, arifes from the different objects we have in view. *I* wrote to fhew what the Annual Gain of the Company amounted to upon a Four Years average of their Current Income and Expenditure: *He* writes to fhew how much in four years they

they have bettered their fituation, without attending to the nature of the articles which promote or diminifh the improvement. In *his* way of treating the fubject, *actual difburfements*, and no other, ought to be charged : whereas, *I* am to look for thofe which have been *incurred* during the period in queftion, all of which, whether paid or poftponed, I contend I am entitled to bring forward.

Maintaining, upon this principle, my right to charge whatever annual intereft of debt the Company were actually liable to, I very readily allow that if the next part of the accufation againft me were well founded, I fhould have drawn up my account moft unfairly ; that is to fay, if I had fet down old arrears introduced into the outgoings, and *added them as a part of the current expence.* But examine the fact ; have I done fo ? Turn to my publication (page 4) and you will find thefe words—" From the " Bombay Charges in 1786-7, I have *deducted* " 40 *lacks* (or 464,000l.) becaufe it is ftated, " in a note accompanying the account, to " be *a fum arifing from arrears.*"—Much as I admire the fpirit with which you come
forth

forth to anſwer my letter, I cannot but lament that you did not previouſly condeſcend to read it.

Confining myſelf thus to what was *incurred*, and proving that I have not made the miſtake imputed to me refpecting what was *defrayed*, I will only further beg your attention while I mention one error which I have myſelf diſcovered, and which is this, —The intereſt payable on the Indian debt, during the period in queſtion, I ſtated to have been £1,963,142 ; whereas Mr. Anderfon (Appendix, No. 5) has ſhewn it to be £2,110,785 ; I have therefore charged too little by £147,643.

The reſult then of this inveſtigation into my Statement of the Nett Surplus of Indian Revenue for the Years 1786-7-8-9-90, is, that I have charged *too little* by £147,643, and *too much* by £84,436, The difference is, £63,207, to which amount I have improperly given the Company credit.

The next items which Mr. Anderſon has attacked, relate partly to Trade and partly to Territory ; and I am happy that, while
he

he has fhewn how egregioufly in thefe particulars I have been wrong, he has given me an opportunity of afcertaining, from his own figures, how I may be correctly right. Heaven forbid that I fhould detain you for a moment in the labyrinths of my erroneous calculations, when, by following the Accountant to the Commiffioners for the Affairs of India, I can at once put you into the road to truth.

In *Mr. Anderfon's* ftatement (page 82) the " expences incurred at home on account " of the poffeffions in India," amount to £829,326, and (page 87) the " nett amount realized from the Import Trade, after defraying all charges, dividends, &c. is £400,315." The difference gives, upon thefe articles, a balance againft the Company of £429,011.

In *my* ftatement, the *ten* firft articles of the Dr. fide, and the *four* firft articles on the Cr. fide, include every thing relative to the *Import Trade*, and the *Charges incurred at home on account of the Territorial Poffeffions in India*. Under thefe heads the Company is debited £15,341,710, and credited £14,857,661 ;

C

£14,857,661 ; which leaves a balance againſt them of £484,049. From this deduct the balance ſtated by your Accountant to be againſt them £429,011, and the error committed by me will appear to amount to £55,038.

There remains but one article more in my account to be diſcuſſed, and that is, the ſum of £560,000 for " Loſs on Goods " and Stores," of which ſum, £493,556 is ſtated by your Accountant to be error.

I feel no difficulty in acknowledging that the correction of Mr. Anderſon, in this inſtance, is perfectly right, and that the error aroſe preciſely in the way he mentions. Only let me ſay, that the miſtake did not originate from my mode of making up the account, but from a miſapplication of the materials I had to uſe.— For inſtance, in the Paper before the Houſe of Commons (No. 39, 1791) Goods and Stores are ſtated to be exported in the ſeaſon 1786. To this I annexed the idea, that the ſhips which carried out ſuch goods and ſtores, ſailed in the ſpring of *that year*, and under that impreſſion drew

up

up my ftatement. It appears, however, that in this I was wrong, becaufe what are called the Exports of 1786 are, in truth, all exported in January, February, March, April, May, and June 1787 ; and this my mifapprehenfion has fo highly delighted your Accountant, that, in his anxiety to ridicule my ignorance, he has faved me the trouble of vindicating myfelf againft the only charge which could have given me uneafinefs, namely—the charge of having *defignedly* mifreprefented the affairs of the Company. Having no other fources than the papers delivered to the Houfe of Commons, from which I can procure information, it would be ftrange indeed if my knowledge of the *practice* of the India Houfe were equal to that of Mr. Anderfon, to whom, as your reprefentative, Directors, as well as Clerks, are bound to give every affiftance.

I have thus gone through every article in my ftatement, and will now requeft your attention while I briefly recapitulate what corrections Mr. Anderfon's publication has rendered it neceffary to make :——

In

In the Article of " Lofs on Goods and Stores,'
I have charged too much againft the Company, -   -   -   -   -   £493,556

On the whole of the Articles which relate to the
Import Trade, and the Expences incurred at
home on account of the Territorial Poffeffions,
I have charged too much againft the Company, -   -   -   -   -   -   55,038

£548,594

In the Article of " Nett Surplus
Revenue," I have charged too
little, -   -   -   £147,643
In ditto, too much -   -   84,436

Deduct the difference, to which amount I have
improperly given the Company credit,   63,207

The Error in my General Statement of the
Profit and Lofs of the Eaft India Company for
Four Years is, -   -   -   -   £485,387

It muft, however, be remembered, that
of this fum, no more than £400,851 is a
miftake of mine, for the reafons before explained refpecting £84,436, which I particularly mentioned to be incorrect.

And here, Sir, let me entreat you to paufe
a moment, and to recollect, that the object
of the letter which I laft year took the liberty to adddrefs to you, was exprefsly
ftated

ftated to be, " to bring the *leading points* be-
" fore the public, and not minutely to fcru-
" tinize every figure." Confider next, the
voluminous and complicated accounts from
which my information was to be derived,
and the very peculiar and intricate manner
in which thofe accounts are kept. Confider,
that, whatever doubts or difficulties arofe,
I had none of that official affiftance from
the India Houfe which your Accountant
can command. Confider, that my General
Statement includes an Inveftigation of the
Eaft India Company's Affairs, both in Europe and Afia, during a period of Four
Years, and is drawn from accounts amounting to above One Hundred Millions Ster-
ling * ;—Confider all thefe circumftances,
and then tell me, why, becaufe in fuch an
undertaking I have committed a miftake of
£400,000, you fend out your Champion
to proclaim, that I have brought forward
" *grofs miftatements*," leading to conclufions
" *fo very different from the actual refult!*"

Having done with my Profit and Lofs

* See Mr. Anderfon's Appendix, Nos. 4 and 5. The
Receipts aud Payments at home amount to £53,664,506 ;
The Revenues and Charges abroad, to £50,675,960.

State-

Statement, let me next proceed to that part of Mr. Anderfon's attack which is levelled at my obfervation on the " Encreafed Value of the Goods on hand." In reply to my objection to this being confidered as *Profit* to the Company, your Accountant fays, " It is fufficient to obferve, that an encreafe " of Trade neceffarily requires an encreafed " Stock of Goods to carry it on ;" and he afterwards ftates the Company " to have " encreafed their goods in the warehoufes, in " order to render them *adequate* to the *de-* " *mands of their trade, on its prefent ex-* " *tended fcale.*"

To make this reafoning of Mr. Ander-fon's conclufive, there is but one thing wanting, which is, the *fact* of the Com-pany's Trade having been extended in fuch a manner as to have required the great in-creafe which appears in the Stock of Tea in Warehoufe. As for the Value of India Goods on hand, it is lefs than it was in 1787, (fee No. 38, 1791)

The following papers will fhew the de-gree of credit to which your accountant's argument is entitled :——

AN

AN ACCOUNT of the Quantity and different Sorts of TEA fold between the 1st of March 1787, and the 1st of March 1791 ; diftinguishing the different Sorts fold at the annual Sales between the above Periods.—(*See No. 4, Account publifhed 19th April, 1790.*)

	BOHEA.	CONGOU.	SOUCHONG.	SINGLO.	HYSON.	TOTAL.
	lb.	lb.	lb.	lb.	lb.	lb.
March and September Sales, 1787 - - -	4,419,677	4,519,155	617,030	5,053,643	1,595,401	16,203,906
March and September Sales, 1788 - - -	3,610,836	4,882,972	949,285	3,865,290	1,717,976	15,025,359
March and September Sales, 1789 - - -	3,497,752	6,470,737	1,259,317	3,833,399	1,653,101	16,714,306
* Between 1st March 1790, and 1st March 1791	- - -	- - -	- - -	- - -	- - -	16,028,343

* See No. 26, 1791, in which the different forts are not diftinguifhed.

AN ACCOUNT of the Quantity of TEA remaining unfold the 1st of March 1790 ; diftinguifhing the different Sorts on Hand.—(*No. 2, 19th April, 1790.*)

	BOHEA.	CONGOU.	SOUCHONG.	SINGLO.	HYSON.	TOTAL.
	lb.	lb.	lb.	lb.	lb.	lb.
Tea in Warehoufe unfold 1st March, 1790 - -	9,235,147	3,775,617	544,347	8,412,771	1,751,252	23,689,134

After

After the perufal of the *firft* of thefe papers, I think it will not be contended, that the Company's trade to China has received any very material extenfion within the four years ; but, if you fhould be of opinion that it has, I will beg of you to caft your eyes over the *fecond* of thofe papers, and to obferve the peculiar mode the Company have adopted in confequence of that extenfion. Of the *Congou* and *Souchong*, for which there appears to have been a very encreafing demand, they have provided only *lb*. 4,299,964 ; and of the *Bohea* and *Singlo*, the confumption of which they have found annually to diminifh, they have ftored in their warehoufes no lefs than *lb*. 17,637,918. If Mr. Anderfon means gravely to infift, that the Directors have acted in this manner on purpofe, I fhould imagine they would feel little obliged to him for the compliment ; but, though I think the fact admits of a very different explanation, I can have no object at prefent in difcuffing the point. I have in my account, to prevent all difpute, taken the amount of the Company's goods on hand at their own valuation, and I fhall therefore difmifs this part of the fubject with merely afking, whether the tradefman who encreafes his

ftock

ftock by heaping up articles, the demand for which daily falls off, ought to gain any great degree of credit for the additional contents of his fhop.

I now come to the laft and moft ferious charge* made againft me by your Account-
D ant,

---

* With refpeft to the omiffion of what the Company gain on fending out bullion, &c. to China, I beg to obferve, that this can by no means be brought againft me as an error, becaufe the papers explaining the amount received in China were not before the Houfe of Commons, neither could I ever have feen them till they appeared in Mr. Anderfon's publication. I have, however, no objeftion to adding the fum he fets down, provided he will, on the other hand, make the deduftions which, in this view of the fubjeft, ought to be brought forward. Undoubtedly the Company do, as your Accountant ftates, by obtaining their cargoes with the produce of the goods and bullion they fend out, fave that intereft which they muft pay if the cargoes were obtained for bills drawn upon them ; but we muft alfo confider the length of time they lofe the ufe of the money employed in the purchafe of the goods and bullion fo fent out, and the rate of infurance, or rifk at which they are tranfported ; and this applies equally to goods, &c. exported to India.

The amount of goods, ftores, and bullion, exported to China, from 1785 to 1788, was £ 3,780,799; on which two years intereft (the leaft that can be charged for the time

during

ant, in which I am accufed of having, in my comparative review of the debts of the

during which the company remain out of
their money) at only 4 per cent. is £302,463

The amount of goods, &c. exported to India
in the fame period, was £1,396,554, of
which fum, before any return is made to the
Company, they lofe the ufe at leaft three
years. On this the intereft, at 4 per cent. is 167,586

Infurance on £5,177,353, being the total
amount exported, at 3¼ per cent. 181,207

£651,256

(For the above fums fee Anderfon's Appendix, No. 9.)

From this, however, muft be deducted whatever the Company have under the head of
" Charges of Merchandize," paid for *Loans.*

£300,000 borrowed of the Bank on
Exchequer bills, for four years, at
4 per cent. is - £48,000

£700,000 borrowed of the Bank on
mortgage of annuities, at 4 per
cent. for one year - 28,000

76,000

£575,256

(For thefe fums, the laft of which I have been obliged to
take on eftimate, fee No. 7, printed 17th March, 1790,
and No. 20, 1791.)

The difference between this fum and what Mr. Anderfon
has fet down as Profit on export trade, would only leave a
balance in favour of the Company of £3,545.

Company,

Company, as they ftood in 1786 and 1790, committed an error to no lefs an amount than £1,676,231; and to this Mr. Anderfon chufes to add a very coarfe infinuation, that the error was committed " for the purpofe " of giving a ftatement that fhould appa- " rently fupport the inferences which it " was previoufly intended to exhibit."

The comparifon referred to was publifhed by me in the following form :

COMPARISON between the DEBTS of the EAST INDIA COMPANY, as they ftood in India and China in 1786 and 1790, and as they ftood in England in 1787 and 1791.

Debt in India, 30th April, 1786 £8,097,028
Debt in China, 20th Feb. 1786   510,841
Debt in England, 1ft March,
   1787   -   -   15,443,349
                                    ─────────── £24,051,218
Debt in India, 30th April, 1790 6,878,507
Debt in England, 1ft March,
   1791   -   -   13,978,436
Add more received on £1,000,000
   encreafed ftock, fubfcribed in
   1789-90, at 174 per cent.   740,000
Add debt transferred to England
   from India, remaining due 1ft
   March, 1791   -   2,303,937
                                    ─────────── 23,900,880
         Diminution of debt in four years £   150,338

In

In this ſtatement I have, according to Mr. Anderſon, committed an error of £ 1,676,231, becauſe I ought to have ſet down the debt in India on 30th April 1786, at £ 9,773,805, inſtead of £ 8,097,082, the ſum at which I have taken it. In anſwer to this accuſation I will beg your attention to a plain recital of faɗs.

I moved in the Houſe of Commons for an account of the debts and aſſets as they ſtood at the different ſettlements in India on the 30th April, 1786, and a return was made from the India Houſe, dated 24th March, 1790, ſtating the debts to have amounted to £ 8,097,082.—(See No. 12, printed 24th March, 1790.) Afterwards you moved for a copy of the letter from the Court of Direɗors to the Governor Gene-ral, dated 19th May, 1790.—(See No. 29, papers of 1791.) It is on the 13th para-graph of this letter that Mr. Anderſon aſ-ſumes the amount of the debt in India on the 30th of April, 1786, to have been £ 9,773,805 ; and it is on the official account from the India Houſe, drawn up not quite two months preceding the date of that let-ter, that I aſſume the amount to have been

at

at the fame period £8,097,082. Both of thefe could not be right: the queftion is, which of them was entitled to the preference.

It pleafes Mr. Anderfon to fay, that if it be fuppofed I had read the 13th paragraph in this letter from the Court of Directors, it would follow I had committed an error on purpofe; and, as I certainly did read this 13th paragraph, it might feem that I ought to plead guilty. Before, however, I receive fentence, I beg I may be allowed to ftate, that previous to feeing the 13th paragraph, I faw the 12th, which, when you have perufed, you will, I think, admit, either that your Accountant reads backwards, and, therefore, though he got as far as 13, never reached 12; or that, notwithftanding his extreme averfion to miftatements, he is not over choice in the felection of his materials for forming an accurate opinion.

The 12th paragraph is in thefe words :—
" We doubt not but that if the inveftiga-
" tion of the amount of arrears of every
" defcription were purfued with accuracy,
" a much larger amount of debts would
" appear

" to have been owing in 1786 than we have
" any where computed upon ; *but the mate-*
" *rials before us are too defective to enable us*
" *to go through such an investigation in a sa-*
" *tisfactory manner.* The confequence, how-
" ever, of the omiffion of arrears has oblig-
" ed us, in the computations we have made
" of the total of our Indian debts, to ftate
" the amount at a later period greater than
" at the former, and *prevents our forming*
" *any accurate opinion of the progreffive ftate*
" *of our affairs in India."*

So much for the authority of the account
to which *Mr. Anderfon* gives a preference ;
and now, Sir, let me beg your attention to
the paper which, on the fame fubject, I have
adopted. It is the official paper delivered
from the India Houfe, unaccompanied by
any doubts or difficulties ; it is figned by
Mr. Wright, Auditor of Indian accounts,
a gentleman who has been too long tried in
that public capacity to be fufpected either
of error or fabrication ; and, which is moft
extraordinary, it is a paper quoted by Mr.
Anderfon himfelf, in ftating the amount of
the *affets* on the 30th April, 1786. It is
plain, therefore, that your Accountant had
                                        read

read it, and it remains for him to give us fome good reafon, why he rather chofe to rely on the opinion of the Court of Directors, founded as they themfelves admit on defective materials, than to adopt an official ftatement for the accuracy of which the vouchers were at hand.

In examining the refults brought forward by Mr. Anderfon in his publication, I fhall have occafion to confider this comparative ftatement of the debts in a different point of view ; for the prefent it is fufficient for me to have fhewn, that the authority I have adopted is fuch as perfectly *juflifies* me in any calculations I may have founded upon it. In truth, if we do not agree that all the accounts, officially figned by the refpective Accountants at home and abroad, are to be affumed as correct, we muft abandon the idea of pretending to inform ourfelves of the ftate of the Company ; in no other way can we have any data to proceed upon, and profit or lofs muft become a matter rather of opinion than figures. To the Eaft India Company themfelves, you will alfo permit me to fay, you have, for the fake of venting a little fpleen againft me, done an effential injury,

injury, and difpofed men to turn with dif-
guft and contempt from the accounts they
annually deliver. What real or fatisfactory
information can be expected from merchants
who, between the months of March and
May 1790, make a difference of £1,670,000,
in ftating the amount of what they owed on
the 30th of April, 1786? and how are we
to place any confidence in what they publifh
as the amount of their debts in 1790, when
they fhew themfelves fo ignorant of what
their fituation was four years antecedent to
that period? There is, Sir, a fufpicious
myftery in all this.—Let us fee what light
we can obtain by examining the ftatement
of the Accountant to the Commiffioners for
the affairs of India.

Expofition of the Fallacy of the Accounts publifhed by the Accountant to the Commiffioners for the Affairs of India, and Remarks upon the Conclufions to be drawn from them.

THE general refult of Mr. Anderfon's review of the Affairs of the Eaft India Company for four years, ending in 1791, is to be found in the fifth chapter of his publication. The four preceding chapters are in that brought to a point, imagined, I confefs, with extreme ingenuity, and fo managed as to affume a very flattering and plaufible appearance.

Your Accountant's object is, to fhew that the improvement in the Company's fituation in four years has amounted to £4,244,336. To prove this, two ftatements are produced ; the *firft* of which affirms that, on a comparifon of debts and affets, as they ftood, at home and abroad, at the commencement and clofe of the period in queftion, there appears the improvement contended for, viz. £4,244,336 ; and the *fecond* explains the actual refources,

from

from which this improvement is fuppofed
to have been derived, to have amounted, in
the four years, to £4,209,962. " The re-
" fults thus drawn," fays Mr. Anderfon,
" from accounts very diftinct from each
" other being fo nearly equal, is a fufficient
" proof of their general correctnefs."

The ftatements being made in this manner to depend upon and confirm each other,
it is plain, that whatever tends to invalidate
either, muft be fatal to both. If I fhew,
that, in the amount of debt faid to be decreafed, there is a moft material error, all
the reft of your figures neceffarily become
faulty ; becaufe, if you are right in the affets, then you muft be wrong in the rc-
fources, and if you are right in the refources, then muft you be wrong in the affets. You have either taken credit for a
certain fum without fhewing how you got
it ; or you have obtained a certain fum
without fhewing how you have difpofed
of it.

I deny that the debts in India have, in
the four years, decreafed in the proportion
your Accountant contends for ; and I affirm,
hat

that his ftatement is erroneous to the amount of £1,594,527. There can be no difficulty in underftanding the iffue between us.

I have before obferved that, in my way of viewing the queftion, I was only entitled to bring forward the regular charges incurred between 1786 and 1790, becaufe my object was to fhew, from an inveftigation of the current income and expenditure of the Company, what, on an average of four years, was the annual fum gained. Whatever was an old claim recovered, ought to have been thrown out of the amount of receipt ; and whatever was a former arrear difcharged, ought to have been excluded from the payments. Accordingly, from the Bombay Charges in 1786-7 I deducted £464,000, becaufe ftated to be a fum arifing from arrears, and I fhould have been equally juftified in rejecting that part of the Receipts from Land Revenue which is defcribed as " Balances of former Years." From the manner in which the accounts are made up it was, however, impracticable to do this, and therefore I have been obliged to give the Company credit for

more

more than their due, by whatever the amount of thofe balances may be.

The ingenuity of Mr. Anderfon has contrived to draw up a ftatement with advantages annexed to it beyond what my imagination, fertile in deception as he feems to confider it, could have conceived. He accufes me of having charged *both the expences incurred, and the expences defrayed,* which, had I done it, certainly would have been a bold meafure, but in point of enterprize and dexterity would, notwithftanding, have fallen infinitely fhort of your Accountant's feat, who has given us what he calls the " Excefs of Revenue," without deducting *either one or the other.* The Intereft incurred on the Debt in India he omits, becaufe it was *not actually paid*; but why the Amount of Arrears which *were defrayed* is alfo kept back, requires confiderable explanation, unlefs you have determined, that the Company fhall neither be charged with what they *ought* to pay, nor what they *do* pay. The amont of Charges defrayed at Bombay in the years 1786-7 was *By. Rs.* 88,04,489*; whereas

* See No. 8, Papers laid before the Houfe, 1791.

Mr.

Mr. Anderſon has taken them at only
By. Rs. 48,04,489 *, and confequently made
the fame deduction that I did, viz. 40 lacks,
or £464,000, *which ſum he has no where brought
to account* I am the more ſurpriſed at this,
becauſe it appears that *he was aware of the
fact relative to theſe Bombay Arrears, and has
mentioned the exact amount in the 49th page of
his publication* ; ſo that, if it be ſuppoſed he
read the firſt part of his work before he
wrote the laſt, it would follow, to ſpeak in his
own ſtyle, that " the error was committed
" for the purpoſe of giving a ſtatement that
" ſhould apparently ſupport the inferences
" which it was previouſly intended to ex-
" hibit."

The " Exceſs of Revenue above the Payments"
  is ſtated by Mr. Anderſon (page 79) at   £3,956,246

Deduct amount defrayed omitted to be charged,   464,000

And the real Exceſs of Revenue above Payments, is   -   -   £3,492,246

The next error to be ſhewn, is in your
Accountant's ſtatement of what has been
ſupplied from the reſources of India to cargoes, &c. (ſee page 80 and 81). This he

* See Mr. Anderſon's Appendix, No. 5.

makes

makes to amount to £4,124,072 ; which is
more than even Mr. Anderſon has ſtated
the exceſs of revenue to have afforded by
£167,826. This difference, which is ab-
ſolutely neceſſary to keep all his machinery
together, and make the ſeparate parts fit,
Mr. A. endeavours, in the following manner, to perſuade us really was ſupplied:—
" Although the Accounts of the Annual
" Revenues of the Provinces in India in-
" clude all the large Articles of Receipt,
" yet various ſmall particulars are omitted,
" which, in the aggregate for ſeveral years,
" afford conſiderable aid to the Indian Re-
" ſources. Theſe conſiſt of *Debts recovered
" from Individuals, Sums overdrawn refunded,*
" *Gain on Remittances, and at the Factories,*
" *Fees paid, &c.* of which, a variety of par-
" ticulars may be found under the heads of
" Extraordinary Receipts in Nos. 27, 28,
" and 34 of the Accounts for 1791, and
" Nos. 1, 2, 3, 4, 5 of thoſe for 1790, printed
" on the 24th of March *."

There is no doubt that, in the papers
referrred to, there are to be found, under
the head of *Extraordinary receipts,* all the

* See Mr. Anderſon's pamphlet, page 78.

par-

particulars mentioned by Mr. Anderfon ;
but, in his exultation at having difcovered
a new refource, he has totally overlooked
the oppofite fide of the account, and omitted to make any mention of the *Extraordinary Difburfements*. The fame docu-
ments which he has quoted fhew thefe to
confift of " *Sundry Adjuftments on Remittances,
Lofs in Mint and on Remittances, Cuftoms refunded, Sundry Balances, Paid on Account of
Fees, Bills paid, Loffes at Factories,*" and a
variety of fmall " *Advances*" in different
departments, (exclufive of the inveftment)
all of which, together, more than counter-
balance the amount obtained by Extra.
Receipts.—I will not fay, this is " a grofs
" miftatement," but I am fure it is a moft
extraordinary overfight in Mr. Anderfon,
to have feen only one fide of the account,
and to have turned away his eyes from
the other.

Thefe two errors rectified will make the
account ftand thus :———

India,

India, by Mr. Anderfon's ftatement, page 81, has, in the four years, fupplied to Cargoes, &c. - - - £4,124,072

And it has been fhewn, that the Excefs of Revenue in four years, deducting £464,000 omitted by Mr. Anderfon, was, £3,492,246

India, therefore, has fupplied more than it produced, and confequently muft have encreafed its debt by, - - - £ 631,826

But it appears by Mr. Anderfon's fhewing, (pages 79, 80) that the "Excefs of Revenue" was obtained by adding the Intereft, payable at Bombay within the four years, to the Principal; and this Intereft, amounting to £670,976, muft certainly have encreafed the debt, - - 670,976

Therefore your Accountant's own ftatements prove an Encreafe of Debt in India, in the four years, - - - £1,302,802

There is however another fum ftill to be added. By No. 27 of the Papers 1791, it appears that the Advances for the Bengal Inveftment in 1789-90 amounted to, *C.Rs.* 1,07,54,912

By Mr. Anderfon's Appendix, No. 6, it appears that the Prime Coft, including Charges, of the Goods fhipped for England in 1789-90 was, 78,57,288

The difference between thefe two fums makes an addition to the debt, - - - 269,762

The Total *Encreafe of the Debt in India in the four years has therefore been*, - - £1,572,564

Now,

Now, in order that the extent of Mr. Anderfon's miftatement may be accurately underftood, I will lay before you his own figures, and, for the fake of the argument, admit them to be correct.———

In his Appendix, No. 1, he ftates the Amount
 of the Debts in India, on the 30th of April
 1786, to be, - - £9,773,805
And on the 30th of April 1790, to be, 7,069,337

Decreafe of Debt in four years, - 2,704,468
In the note to page 52 he ftates the Amount of
 Debt *transferred* from India to England in
 the fame period to be, - - 2,682,505

Your Accountant therefore makes the Amount
 of Debt *paid off* in India in four years to be
 only, - - - - 21,963

But he has himfelf fhewn how every fhilling
 obtained, or even pretended to have been
 obtained, has been difpofed of ; fo that this
 fum, fmall as it is, muft be an error ; and
 adding to it the Amount of New Debt
 which I have proved to have been incurred
 within the four years, - - 1,572,564

Mr. Anderfon *has miflated the Debts of the
Company, in his comparifon of them between
April 1786 and April 1790, by no lefs
than* - - - £1,594,527

      The

The *firſt* part of your Accountant's ſtate-ment being thus proved erroneous to ſo very great an amount, renders it perfectly unneceſſary to inveſtigate the *ſecond* ; from the nature of the accounts it muſt be inac-curate in a correſponding ſum, and it would be an idle waſte of time to enter into a diſ-cuſſion of the various errors out of which that ſum ariſes.

But, though *I* am not called upon to en-quire further, *you* are bound to take care that your Accountant ſhould immediately come forward, and afford the public ſatis-faction upon an error of ſuch material im-port as that which I have pointed out. You will be pleaſed to obſerve that *Mr. Ander-ſon*, if he has been right in ſtating the debts in 1786 at £ 9,773,805, has *detected the Company* in miſrepreſenting their debts in 1790 by no leſs than £ 1,594,527 ; and the *Auditor of Indian Accounts*, if he was right in ſtating their debts in 1790 at £ 7,069,337, *convicts the Accountant to the Commiſſioners for the Affairs of India* of hav-ing officially given a falſe credit to the Com-pany of £ 1,594,527. This, Sir, is ſo very myſterious a buſineſs that no time ought to be be loft in explaining it. If I am any thing like correct in my figures, it is obvious that either the Company have deceived you, or you, by your Accountant, have mifled the public. The readinefs with which I have met the inveftigation of Mr. Anderfon on every point where he has attacked *my* ftatement, will, I truft, fuggeft to you the neceffity of defending *your* accounts in a fimilar manner; for furely that explanation which pride tells a private gentleman he owes to his own character, a fenfe of duty will convince the Board of Controul they cannot refufe to enter into. Do not, however, miftake me, and fuppofe that I am inviting a controverfy, fince I can with much truth affure you that nothing is further from my intentions than again to interfere on this fubject. I conceived myfelf bound to defend the ftatement which I originally publifhed and the grounds on which I reft my vindication being now laid before the public (who will make their own comments upon them) I have done with Eaft India accounts. There is nothing very feducing in the ftudy of Indian papers, and, as I have no natural difpofition to act as eftablifhed cenfor over the Company, I leave

F 2   it

it to thofe to watch their future operations who, from parliamentary fituation, fhall feel it to be incumbent upon them fo to do.

But it might feem as if I were inclined to treat Mr. Anderfon as cavalierly as he has treated all thofe gentlemen who have written on the other fide of the queftion, if I were to conclude without taking fome fur-notice of his pamphlet. Let me, therefore, having fhewn wherein he is wrong, haften to avail myfelf of his fuperior intelligence on thofe points, where I bow to his autho-rity, and acknowledge him to have afforded us moft important information.

Mr. Anderfon has enabled us correctly to afcertain, what the value of the territories in India is, confidered as an eftate—what the advantage is which the Company derive from the poffeffion of that eftate—what the fitu-ation of the proprietors of India ftock would be upon a general fettlement of their affairs —and, laftly, what ground there is to ima-gine that Parliament will take the territo-ries, and fecure their prefent dividend of 8 per cent. to the Proprietors.

The

The nett revenues of India are ftated by Mr. Anderfon to have amounted in the four years to (a) - - £ 3,956,246

But as this was procured by poftponing the payment of the annual intereft incurred on the Bombay debt, the amount of the intereft fo poftponed muft, in this view of the fubject, be deducted, in order to fhew the value of India as an eftate.—Deduct therefore (b) - - - 670,976

Surplus Revenue in India £ 3,285,270

Deduct " Expences incurred at home on account of the poffeffions in India" (c) 893,226

The nett value of the Company's eftate in India in four years was - - £ 2,392,044
Or per ann. - - £598,011

(d) The quantity of Indian goods fold in the four years amounted to - - £ 7,966,715
(d) Their prime coft and feveral charges of freight, cuftoms, &c. to - - 7,560,233

406,482

Add to this the amount which Mr. Anderfon ftates the Revenues of India to have furnifhed in thefe four years to the aid of the Company's treafuries, or the payment of commercial charges, over and above all the expences incurred at home on account of the territorial poffeffions (e) - 3,230,846

The apparent advantage derived from India was - - - £ 3,637,328

√

(a) Anderfon, page 79. (b) Ditto, page 79-80. (c) Ditto, page 81-2.
d) Ditto, page 86. (e) Ditto, page 83-4.

Carried forward £ 3,637,328

Brought forward   £3,637,328

From this, however, muſt be deducted—

(a) Indian goods in warehouſe 1ſt
March 1787   -   £1,158,617
Ditto, ditto, ditto, 1ſt
March 1791   -   826,842

Value of goods in warehouſe leſs
1791 than 1787   -   £331,775
(b) The cargo of the Houghton not
brought to account   -   113,550
(c) Half the expences incurred for
St. Helena   -   -   57,355
(b) Half the amount of freight incurred more than charged againſt the
goods ſold   -   -   240,017
(b) Half a debt incurred in the de-
partment of ſhipping   -   6,262
(b) Intereſt on bills drawn from
India   -   -   -   8,829
(d) Half of the Intereſt incurred
on Bonds   -   -   205,258
(e) Three Years Intereſt, at 4 per
Cent. on £1,396,554, Prime

(a) Papers of 1791, No. 38.   (b) Anderſon, page 88.   (c) Ditto 87.
(d) Anderson's Appendix, No. 3 and 4.

(e) Theſe articles are taken arbitrarily, and may be ſubject to altera-
tion in favour of a greater or leſs ſum. Reſpecting the Inſurance, I
apprehend there can be no material difference of opinion, and as to the
three years Intereſt on the Prime Coſt of Goods &c. I cannot ſee how
leſs can be charged from the time of the firſt Inveſtiture of the money advanced for them, and the realizing their Produce from the ſales of the
goods procured by them in India. The total Amount would be £167,586
but I have deducted one half of what the Company are ſuppoſed to have
paid for *loans*, under *charges of merchandize*; (vide ante page 18). The
Articles I have ſet down at *half*, are thoſe of which it was impoſſible to
diſtinguiſh what proportion ought to be charged to *China*, and what to
India.

Carried forward   £963,945   £3,637,328

Brought forward, £963,045 £3,637,328

Coft of Goods, &c. exported to India in the four years, -	125,586	
(b) Infurance out on ditto, at 3¼ per Cent. - -	48,879	
(b) Infurance home on £4,183,830, being the Prime Coft of Goods Sold and the Houghton's Cargo, at 3½ per Cent, -	146,434	
Total to be deducted, -		1,283,944

Apparent Balance in Favor of the Company, £2,353,384 ✓

But, to obtain this Balance, it has been ſhewn that a Debt was incurred in India amounting to, - - - £1,594,527 ✓

The actual Advantage, therefore, derived by the Company from their Poffeffions in India in four years was, - - £ 758,857 ✓

Or, on the average, per Annum, 189,714 ✓

It is from this ſum the proprietors ought to have regulated their dividend, and when the capital they employ is confidered, and the ſum that ought to be ſet apart to an-ſwer contingencies is eſtimated, I leave it to any honeſt merchant to decide what that dividend ought to have been, or whether there ought to have been any.

(a) The

Situation of the Proprietors on a General Settlement of their Affairs. (a) The Debt due in India, 30th April 1790, £7,069,337

(b) The Debt due in England (exclusive of the Capital Stock) on the 1st of March 1791, - - - 8,978,436

(b) Debt transferred from India to England, due 1st of March 1791, - - 2,189,336

Total of Debts to be discharged before the Proprietors are entitled to make any Dividend amongst themselves, - - £18,237,109

To discharge this, they had
    (a) Assets in India, 30th April 1790, - - £ 6,265,221
    (a) Assets in China, 14th Feb. 1790, - - 79,241
    Assets in England, 1st March 1791, - - £13,607,575

19,952,037

So that the Proprietors who have subscribed to the Capital Stock £5,748,000, would have to divide amongst them, - - £ 1,714,928

That this loss of Four Millions must fall upon *the Proprietors*, Mr. Anderson has very correctly explained when, speaking of the Capital Stock, he properly observes, that " the value of each respective share

---

(a) Anderson's Appendix, No. 1.

(b) Appendix, No. 2. The Capital Stock is called £ 5,000,000, but the rate at which it was subscribed makes the real Amount paid by the Proprietors £ 5,748,000.

" must

" muft depend altogether on the balance
" which fhall remain after the difpofal of
" their property, and the payment of their
" feveral debts (*a*)."

Still the title of *Bankrupts* cannot, in ftrict-
nefs, be applied to the Eaft India Company,
upon the foregoing ftatement, becaufe the
lofs is limited to the Proprietors, and there
appears fufficient to anfwer the demands of
the Creditors. You are, however, to recollect, that, in the preceding account
I have taken Mr. Anderfon's word for
the Amount of the Debts, and affumed
the Affets to be convertible into the fum at
which they are valued by the Company.
But, if it be not too much to fay that (*b*)
10 *per Cent.* is a lofs reafonably to be expected upon the realization of the value of
the effects in queftion, the Company would
appear to be in a ftate of actual infolvency,
and that too without mentioning the
£ 1,594,527, which, if Mr. Anderfon has
been accurate in his publication, ought certainly to be added to the amount of their
debts.

To counteract any bad effects which
might arife from this gloomy view of the

G   fubject,

subject, a more flattering prospect has lately been held out to us. It has been insinuated, that *Parliament would take from the Company their Territorial Posses-sions, and secure to the Proprietors the present Dividend of* 8 *per Cent.* The Accountant to the Commissioners for the Affairs of India has enabled us thoroughly to examine the probability of this. I will only assume, on the one hand, that the *Expence of the War in India will create a debt of five millions,* and, on the other, that *the Territorial Possessions are worth ten years purchase:* every other figure shall be accurately copied from Mr. Anderson.

(a) See Anderson, page 31.

(b) I have stated the loss on the Assets in this manner, because it is most easily to be comprehended, and the object here is not to prove to what extent the Company may be infolvent, but merely to shew that they are so. If a complete investigation was to be entered into, the value of the Company's Assets would be reduced at least 40 per Cent. Immense losses would arise on the advances to the manufacturers in India, the Debts outstanding (particularly that from the Nabob of Arcot) the Stores and Export Goods in India, the value of Goods in Warehouse at home, the value of the India House, Warehouses, Ships, Claims on Government for Manilla expedition, &c. &c. &c.

The

The nett value of the Company's Eftate in
India has been fhewn to be £598,011 per
ann. which at 10 years purchafe would
be worth   -   -   -   £5,980,110

But as it fhall be fuppofed that Government
are to adopt the whole of what the Company poffefs in India, their affets there fhall
be added, and that too even at their own
valuation   -   -   -   6,265,221

The utmoft value of what the Company have
to fell in India is   -   -   £12,245,331

Now, it is expected, as the confideration
of being put into poffeffion of thefe valu-
able premifes, that the public fhould take
upon themfelves the following debts:

The debt in India   -   -   £7,069,337
The transferred debt, which Mr. Dundas has
declared muft always be confidered as following and being a burthen on the territories   -   -   -   (a) 1,189,336
The debt incurred by the prefent war efti-
mated as low as   -   -   5,000,000

Therefore the price expected is   -   13,248,673
And the (b) utmoft value of the thing is   12,245,331

The price more than the value   £1,003,342

G 2   I am

(a) As the five millions new debt is affumed up to this day, the amount
of the transferred debt difcharged at home fince 1791 is, to the amount of
a million, deducted.

(b) With refpect to the value of what the Company call their *dead ftock*,
I confider it as being a part of the territory. It chiefly confifts of *build-
ings*

I am afraid you would think I laughed at you, if I were to afk, whether you could ever ferioufly propofe to give fuch a premium for an incumbrance ; and ftill more fhould I fear offending you by talking about an annuity of 8 per cent. to be fecured to the Proprietors of India ftock as an addition to the bargain. It may not, however, be improper to obferve, that if any advantage arifing from conqueft in the prefent war fhould be fuggefted, as adding to the value of the Company's poffeffions in India, it will be neceffary, before the argument can have any weight, to fhew that the new acquifitions produce a nett income of £500,000 ; otherwife they will not pay the intereft at which the five millions expended has been obtained.

Thefe, Sir, are the general conclufions which Mr. Anderfon's publication has enabled us to form, and if, in fubftance, they are correct, it is obvious that the whole reliance of the Eaft India Company muft be placed upon the *China trade,* as the only

ings and *fortifications,* which even if it were practicable to fell them feparately, could not be fold without deftroying the value of the Company's eftate. They are in truth the beft *title deeds* they poffefs.

fource

fource from which they can hope for relief. The nature of that trade, its operation, and confequences, are fubjects foreign to the prefent difcuffion. It is fufficient for me to obferve that, at any rate, it cannot be looked upon as a very permanent affiftance to the Company, becaufe if, in a national point of view, it is detrimental, no partiality for any particular body of men ought to encourage its continuance; and, if it be fraught with general advantage, there can be no pretence for vefting it in individuals as a monopoly. The exclufion of Ireland from this branch of commerce is, particularly, fuch an act of injuftice as no arguments can reafonably defend, and perhaps no meafures, for any great length of time, effect.

It is to the ftate of the Company as *connected with India* that we muft turn our attention, when the renewal of the charter comes into queftion : and a moft important and ferious difcuffion it will afford. The minds of men have been worked up to a pitch of extravagant expectation, with regard to fome advantages which are fuppofed to be near at hand. On what thofe expectations

pectations are built, I know not, but this I am sure of, that it will add but little to the credit of the House of Commons, if they seperate this session without taking some steps to inform themselves of the Company's real situation. The year is perhaps too far advanced to investigate their extensive concerns in all their various branches, and finally to decide upon the fate of the Charter: such a work would require more labour and attention than, possibly, at this time can be spared. But I am certain that a Committee, appointed by Parliament, might, in one week, produce a report abundantly sufficient to elucidate and ascertain all those *leading points* which must serve as the foundation of future arrangements. Let such a Committee be fairly and impartially appointed, and the East India Company will, in a few days, appear, either a great and opulent body entitled to respect and confidence, or a society of speculative adventurers, themselves catching at, or holding out to others, an empty bubble. It will be seen too, whether the object of those who support them, be commercial advantage to the nation, or extensive patronage to themselves.

If the Commiffioners for the Affairs of India, at the head of whom you fo ably prefide, ftill feel confident in the ftrength and accuracy of thofe accounts which they have, by their Accountant, given to the Public, they can have no objection to the appointment of fuch a Committee ; if not, we muft continue in doubt, whether the Company be thriving, or bankrupts ; and all we can be certain of will be, that the patronage which, through the medium of the Court of Directors, Adminiftration enjoys, is found quite great enough to fatisfy their prefent demands, and much too great to be expofed to the hazard of any inveftigation.

I have the honour to be,

&c. &c. &c.